Also by Jaroslaw Jankowski

Why Are We So Different?
Your Guide to the 16 Personality Types

Why are we so very different from one another? Why do we organise our lives in such disparate ways? Why are our modes of assimilating information so varied? Why are our approaches to decision-making so diverse? Why are our forms of relaxing and 'recharging our batteries' so dissimilar?

Your Guide to the 16 Personality Types will help you to understand both yourselves and other people better. It will aid you not only in avoiding any number of traps, but also in making the most of your personal potential, as well as in taking the right decisions about your education and career and in building healthy relationships with others. The book contains the ID16™© Personality Test, which will enable you to determine your own personality type. It also offers a comprehensive description of each of the sixteen types.

The Mentor

Your Guide
to the INFJ Personality Type

The ID16$^{TM©}$ Personality Types series

JAROSLAW JANKOWSKI
M.Ed., EMBA

LOGOS MEDIA

This is a book which can help you exploit your potential more fully, build healthy relationships with other people and make the right decisions about your education and career. However, it should not be considered to be a substitute for expert physiological or psychiatric consultation. Neither the author nor the publisher accept any responsibility whatsoever for any detrimental effects which may result from the inappropriate use of this book.

ID16™© is an independent typology developed by Polish educator and manager Jaroslaw Jankowski and grounded in Carl Gustav Jung's theory. It should not be confused with the personality typologies and tests proposed by other authors or offered by other institutions.

Original title: Twój typ osobowości: Mentor (INFJ)
Translated from the Polish by Caryl Swift
Proof reading: Lacrosse | experts in translation
Layout editing by Zbigniew Szalbot

Published by LOGOS MEDIA

Paperback: ISBN 978-83-7981-081-9
EPUB: ISBN 978-83-7981-082-6
MOBI: ISBN 978-83-7981-083-3

Contents

Preface

The work in your hands is a compendium of knowledge on the *mentor*. It forms part of the *ID16*TM© *Personality Types* series, which consists of sixteen books on the individual personality types and *Who Are You? The ID16*TM© *Personality Test*, an introduction to the ID16TM© independent personality typology, which is based on the theory developed by Carl Gustav Jung.

As you explore this book on the *mentor*, you will find the answer to a number of crucial questions:

- How do *mentors* think and what do they feel? How do they make decisions? How do they solve problems? What makes them anxious? What do they fear? What irritates them?
- Which personality types are they happy to encounter on their road through life and

which ones do they avoid? What kind of friends, life partners and parents do they make? How do others perceive them?

- What are their vocational predispositions? What sort of work environment allows them to function most effectively? Which careers best suit their personality type?
- What are their strengths and what do they need to work on? How can they make the most of their potential and avoid pitfalls?
- Which famous people correspond to the *mentor*'s profile?

The book also contains the most essential information about the ID16$^{TM©}$ typology.

We sincerely hope that it will help you in coming to know yourself and others better.

ID16™© and Jungian Personality Typology

ID16™© numbers among what are referred to as Jungian personality typologies, which draw on the theories developed by Carl Gustav Jung (1875-19161), a Swiss psychiatrist and psychologist and a pioneer of the 'depth psychology' approach.

On the basis of many years of research and observation, Jung came to the conclusion that the differences in people's attitudes and preferences are far from random. He developed a concept which is highly familiar to us today: the division of people into extroverts and introverts. In addition, he distinguished four personality functions, which form two opposing pairs: sensing-intuition and thinking-feeling. He also established that one function is dominant in each pair. He became convinced that each and every person's dominant functions are fixed and independent of external conditions and that, together, what they form is a personality type.

In 1938, two American psychiatrists, Horace Gray and Joseph Wheelwright, created the first personality test based on Jung's theories. It was designed to make it possible to determine the dominant functions within the three dimensions described by Jung, namely, **extraversion-introversion**, **sensing-intuition** and **thinking-feeling**. That first test became the inspiration for other researchers. In 1942, again in America, Isabel Briggs Myers and Katherine Briggs began using their own personality test, broadening Gray's and Wheelwright's classic, three-dimensional model to include a fourth: **judging-perceiving**. The majority of subsequent personality typologies and tests drawing on Jung's theories also take that fourth dimension into account. They include the American typology published by David W. Keirsey in 1978 and the personality test developed in the nineteen seventies by Aušra Augustinavičiūtė, a Lithuanian psychologist. Over the following decades, other European researchers followed in their footsteps, creating more four-dimensional personality typologies and tests for use in personal coaching and career counselling.

ID16$^{TM©}$ figures among that group. An independent typology developed by Polish educator and manager Jaroslaw Jankowski, it was published in the first decade of the twenty-first century. ID16$^{TM©}$ is based on Carl Jung's classic theory and, like other contemporary Jungian typologies, it follows a four-dimensional path, terming those dimensions the **four natural inclinations**. These inclinations are dichotomous in nature and the picture they provide gives us information regarding a person's personality type. Analysis of the first inclination is intended to determine the dominant **source of life energy**, this being either the exterior or the interior world. Analysis of the second inclination defines the dominant **mode of assimilating information**, which occurs via the senses or via intuition. Analysis of the third inclination supplies a description of the **decision-making mode**, where either mind or heart is dominant, while analysis of the fourth inclination produces a definition of the dominant **lifestyle** as either organised or spontaneous. The combination of all these natural inclinations results in **sixteen possible personality types**.

One remarkable feature of the ID16™© typology is its practical dimension. It describes the individual personality types in action – at work, in daily life and in interpersonal relations. It neither concentrates on the internal dynamics of personality nor does it undertake any theoretical attempts at explaining or commenting on invisible, interior processes. The focus is turned more toward the ways in which a given personality type manifests itself externally and how it affects the surrounding world. This emphasis on the social aspect of personality places ID16™© somewhat closer to the previously mentioned typology developed by Aušra Augustinavičiūtė.

Each of the ID16™© personality types is the result of a given person's natural inclinations.

There is nothing evaluative or judgemental about ascribing a person to a given type, though. No particular personality type is 'better' or 'worse' than any other. Each type is quite simply different and each has its own potential strengths and weaknesses. ID16$^{TM©}$ makes it possible to identify and describe those differences. It helps us to understand ourselves and discover our place in the world.

Familiarity with our personality profile enables us to make full use of our potential and work on the areas which might cause us trouble. It is an invaluable aid in everyday life, in solving problems, in building healthy relationships with other people and in making decisions relating to our education and careers.

Determining personality is a process which is neither arbitrary nor mechanical in nature. As the 'owner and user' of our personality, each and every one of us is fully capable of defining which type we belong to. The individual's role is thus pivotal. This self-identification can be achieved either by analysing the descriptions of the ID16$^{TM©}$ personality types and steadily narrowing down the fields of choice or by taking the short cut provided by the ID16$^{TM©}$ Personality Test.[1] The role played by each 'personality user' is equally crucial when it comes to the test, given that the outcome depends entirely on the answers they provide.

---

[1] The test can be found in *Why Are We So Different? Your Guide to the 16 Personality Types* by Jaroslaw Jankowski.

Identifying personality types helps us to know both ourselves and others. Nonetheless, it should not be treated as some kind of future-determining oracle. No personality type can ever justify our weaknesses or poor interpersonal relationships. It might, however, help us to understand their causes!

ID16™© treats personality type not as a static, genetic, pre-determined condition, but as a product of innate and acquired characteristics. As such, it is a concept which neither diminishes free will nor engages in pigeonholing people. What it does is open up new perspectives for us, encouraging us to work on ourselves and indicating the areas where that work is most needed.

The Mentor (INFJ)

The Personality in a Nutshell

Life motto: The world CAN be a better place!

In brief, *mentors* ...

are creative and sensitive. With their gaze fixed firmly on the future, they spot opportunities and potential imperceptible to others. Idealists and visionaries, they are geared towards helping people and are conscientious, responsible and, at one and the same time, courteous, caring and friendly. They strive to understand the mechanisms governing the world and view problems from a wide perspective.

Superb listeners and observers, *mentors* are characterised by their extraordinary empathy, intuition and trust of people and are capable of reading the feelings and emotions of others. They find criticism and conflict difficult to bear and can come across as enigmatic.

The *mentor's* four natural inclinations:

- source of life energy: the interior world
- mode of assimilating information: intuition
- decision-making mode: the heart
- lifestyle: organised

Similar personality types:

- the Idealist
- the Counsellor
- the Enthusiast

Statistical data:

- *mentors* constitute one per cent of the global community and are the most rarely occurring of the sixteen personality types
- women predominate among *mentors* (80 per cent)
- Norway is an example of a nation corresponding to the *mentor's* profile[2]

---

[2] What this means is not that all the residents of Norway fall within this personality type, but that Norwegian society as a whole possesses a great many of the character traits typical of the *mentor*.

The Four-Letter Code

In terms of Jungian personality typology, the universal four-letter code for the *mentor* is INFJ.

General character traits

Mentors may be the most rarely occurring of the sixteen personality types, but they have an enormous influence on the fates of other people and, indeed, of the world. They perceive things which are far from evident to others, seeing the connections between disparate events and identifying repeated patterns of behaviour. When working to solve problems, they analyse the situation from various angles and different perspectives. As a rule, they are capable of foreseeing the possible development of events and identifying the potential opportunities and dangers in a given set of circumstances.

They are also aware that another world exists, a world which can only be construed through intuition or faith. The spiritual dimension of life is frequently more important to them than the material one perceived via the senses.

Interior compass

By nature, *mentors* are idealists and they are usually characterised by their extremely high moral standards and ethical conduct. They will often ponder over how to make the most of their life's potential and they thirst both to improve themselves and to help other people find their place in the world, convinced that it is the natural duty of every human being to assist others and stand in the defence of the less powerful and those who are unable to look after their own interests. With their longing to meliorate the world, solve its problems and help people to develop, they believe that, if only everyone made a genuine effort to understand others, life would be easier and the world would be a much better place. When they involve themselves in something, they do so because they are aware that there is an issue to be solved and not for the sake of their careers or prospective honours.

Mentors may be visionaries, but they are also activists. Not content with concepts alone, they strive to breathe life into their ideas and have a sense that they are always 'on call', being ever at the ready to launch into action and take up the cudgels to defend those who are the victims of oppression. Their lives are guided by a clear aim: they have an extremely powerful conviction as to what is important and what needs to be done and there is little that can stop them from accomplishing their visions.

Mentors will often invoke a range of theories or concepts. Drawn to the world of the spirit, they have a liking for symbol and metaphor. At the same time, a host of widely accepted forms of behaviour and customs strike them as utterly devoid of sense and they struggle to come to terms with the fact that other people see them in a different light.

Perception

Mentors hunger for a better understanding of the world. They reflect on the meaning and sense of life and are absorbed by questions of a philosophical and/or religious nature. Intent observers, they endeavour to fit all the new information and data they acquire into their internal picture of the world. If that proves impossible, they will acknowledge that either that picture or their outlook might need rearranging or restructuring.

This internal process, invisible to the eyes of others, is something they engage in throughout their lives. Their minds are constantly at work in top gear and they are scrupulous in their analysis of new data. Today's world, where people are bombarded by an ever increasing volume of information, frequently sends *mentors* into overload. They try to cope with the sheer mass of the data coming their way by reducing it, ignoring things which are similar to something they have already assimilated.

As others see them

Other people see *mentors* as extremely warm, friendly and likeable, while their wisdom and creative approach to problems arouse widespread respect. On the other hand, they are highly intuitive and their personalities are complex, which makes them difficult to get to know and challenging to fathoming out. Indeed, they can give the impression of being both puzzling and mysterious; they have their own world and they guard it against others. The only people they will allow into it are those closest to them – but they can still come up with a number of surprises even for their nearest and dearest! Moreover, there are some aspects of their personalities which they themselves find baffling.

Given that they need solitude and calm in order to 'recharge their batteries', *mentors* will sometimes withdraw to the sidelines, though this is not to say that they keep people at a distance. On the contrary, they continue to show them warmth and take a genuine interest in them. They surround those closest to them with particular solicitude and will always make every effort to ensure that no one hurts or harms them.

Communication

In general, *mentors* are past masters of the spoken and written word. Capable of expressing their thoughts clearly, they communicate superbly with others. However, they are often averse to speaking in public, although they cope extremely well when forced to do so. They are also outstanding listeners and observers, not only decoding what other people say, but also reading their gestures and feelings. Being well aware of the immense power of words, they are usually able to keep the language they use under firm control and are equally as capable of remaining silent if they believe it to be for the best.

Mentors are unstinting in their praise and themselves enjoy the compliments of others. On the other hand, they find criticism hard to cope with, often taking it as a personal attack. Excessive bureaucracy and formalism irritate them immensely; however, they also dislike the kind of familiarity manifest in back-slapping, shoulder clapping and other forms of physical contact during a conversation.

Thinking

Mentors often reflect on the purpose of their life and on what they want to achieve in it, and they may well reassess their priorities and formulate them anew. They are often plagued by an inner sense of anxiety: with so many ideas, they will never succeed in bringing all of them to fruition and they frequently upbraid themselves for not making the very most of their capabilities and potential, or for not doing more for others.

With their ability to foresee future opportunities and dangers, the present serves them not as a goal, but as a springboard. In general, their eyes are fixed firmly on the future and they have no real perception of their previous achievements; indeed, they often remain unaware of just how much they have already accomplished. For *mentors*, the horizon is always teeming with fresh needs to be met and new tasks to be tackled.

Decisions

When confronted with the need to make a decision, *mentors* not only need time to weigh up the various possible solutions, but peace, quiet and, for preference, seclusion while they do so. Their ideas are often unconventional. They dislike conflict, but if they recognise that it will have positive results, they will not go out of their way to avoid it.

Order is something they prize greatly and they will struggle to function in surroundings where chaos holds sway. Before they set about doing something, they devote a good deal of energy and time to gathering the requisite information and establishing the best way of going about it. As a rule, they let their intuition be their guide and trust in their presentiments, a *modus operandi* which can sometimes lead to their neglecting other people's opinions or digging their heels in and sticking to their own view.

In the face of stress

Mentors are susceptible to stress. Often plagued by an inner tension, they frequently find it well nigh impossible to relax. This, in turn, can give rise to somatic problems such as high blood pressure. When they do succeed in tearing themselves away from their commitments, they prefer to relax in peace, in the company of their nearest and dearest and "far from the madding crowd".

Socially

Mentors have deep and complex personalities. At the same time, though, they are friendly and display enormous warmth towards others. They have no liking for convention or courteous gestures and derive no enjoyment from superficial relationships. Forging a friendship with people whose behaviour goes against their convictions or who try to give the impression of being something other than they are is beyond their capabilities.

They often have a talent for leadership, despite not being people of the leader-cum-showman ilk, since they neither seek the spotlight nor pursue recognition. Nonetheless, they are capable of exercising an extraordinary influence on other people. They are outstanding mentors ... hence the name for this personality type. Given their talent for spurring others to start looking at the world and their own situation in new ways, people find meeting them and talking to them to be a source of inspiration and a motivating force.

With their genuine interest in other people's problems, their ability to listen and their remarkable intuition, they make outstanding advisors and therapists. Their relationships with others are extremely direct and personal and they are not deceived by appearances, but have the gift of reading other people's real feelings and emotions, even when those people themselves are unconscious of them.

Amongst friends

Mentors seek natural, profound relationships. They value sincerity and authenticity and their commitment is absolute and limitless, on occasions even to the point where their critical faculties are suspended. Their ability to control their emotions and their need for solitude mean that strangers can sometimes make the mistake of perceiving them as distanced from their surroundings, whereas, in fact, they have an enormous liking for people and good interpersonal relationships matter to them greatly. They are faithful friends and, believing that true friendships make life better, they are ready to invest immense effort and energy in nurturing and improving their own.

Although they shun the pursuit of popularity, they are usually widely liked. People appreciate not only their friendly attitude, honesty and creative approach to their tasks, but also the fact that they help others to identify and make the most of their potential. They themselves are happiest amongst people who understand them and who accept and respect them for who they are.

Their circle tends to include representatives of well-nigh all the sixteen personality types. However, they most frequently strike up a friendship with *idealists*, *counsellors*, *protectors* and other *mentors* and, most rarely, with *animators*, *practitioners* and *administrators*. In general, their friendships are few, but their relationships with the people closest to them are profound and long-lasting.

As life partners

Mentors make highly devoted and caring partners. Their feelings run deep and they frequently see their relationship with their partner as something mystical and spiritual, yearning for that complete union of heart and mind which will allow them to share their most profound feelings, experiences, dreams and visions.

Demonstrative of their love themselves, they, too, enjoy gestures and expressions of affection and long for that perfect union, an attitude which means that they are not only devoted to their partner, but are also ready and willing to work at their relationships. However, when taken to extremes, it is an approach which can often prove wearing and frustrating for their partner, who may well fear that they are incapable of meeting those high expectations. It might also happen that *mentors* will seek their ideal outside their relationship.

The natural candidates for a *mentor's* life partner are people of a personality type akin to their own: *idealists*, *counsellors* or *enthusiasts*. Building mutual understanding and harmonious relations will be easier in a union of that kind. Nonetheless, experience has taught us that people are also capable of creating happy and successful relationships despite what would seem to be an evident typological incompatibility. Moreover, the differences between two partners can lend added dynamics to a relationship and engender personal development.

As parents

The role of parent comes as naturally to *mentors* as breathing and they take it extremely seriously. Loving and devoted, they are ready to give their children their all, demonstrating warmth and tenderness in abundance and, as a rule, enjoying close and profound relationships with them. They also take the time to explain to them how the world works, desiring to bring them up to be independent adults, capable of thinking and deciding for themselves, forming their own opinions and distinguishing good from bad. They go about this by allowing their offspring to take part in making a range of decisions, motivating them to learn and encouraging them to make the most of their talents and gifts. However, they also make high demands of them and are capable of severity.

Their offspring trust them immensely and will thus readily turn to them for help with their problems. They will sometimes resent the fact that they have to make much more of an effort than some of their peers; however, as adults, they are grateful to their *mentor* parents for demanding that of them and appreciate the way that they taught them to lead good lives and encouraged them to make the most of their talents and do something concrete with their enthusiasms.

Work and career paths

When they can see the sense of what they are doing, *mentors* have the ability to work hard and are ready to devote themselves to the task in hand. Whatever it may be, they will strive to accomplish it to the highest possible standard. Given their aversion to crowds and superficial interpersonal relationships, they are happiest working independently or in small groups.

As part of a team

Mentors dislike conflict, confrontation and antagonism, believing that harmonious collaboration and a friendly atmosphere are the best guarantees of success. They themselves bring that atmosphere to a team and they are often the people who will help others both to take a wider view of problems and to attain success.

When it comes to their superiors, they appreciate strong leaders who act in accordance with their ideals and, at one and the same time, support the people they supervise.

Aims

Mentors enjoy helping others to solve problems. To that end, they employ an approach which involves inducing them to ask the right questions and then seek the answers. The knowledge that they are being of some assistance gives them enormous satisfaction and, with their unshakeable belief that they can have an impact on the destiny of their country and, indeed of the world, they set themselves ambitious goals. While aims of that ilk might well strike other people as high-flown or simply unrealistic, *mentors* themselves take them extremely seriously.

Companies and institutions

Mentors fit in well in companies or institutions which are geared towards establishing equal opportunities, supporting the local community or helping people who are unable to cope with their problems. As such, they often find their niche in welfare and other social work, in counselling or consultancy and in education. They also make good writers and members of the clergy.

Often the minds behind all kinds of systemic solutions, including those related to the life of society, they are in their element in any position which demands creativity and provides them with independence of action.

Tasks

Mentors enjoy tasks which enable them to help other people and change the world for the better. On the other hand, they are at a loss when faced with the necessity of carrying out administrative work which requires meticulous attention to elaborate detail, the analysis of documents or the processing of data, and are equally as confounded when it comes to operating in situations involving a conflict of interests or performing a job which goes against their outlook on the world.

Professions

Knowledge of our own personality profile and natural preferences provides us with invaluable help in choosing the optimum path in our professional careers. Experience has shown that, while *mentors* are perfectly able to work and find fulfilment in a range of fields, their personality type naturally predisposes them to the following fields and professions:

- advisor
- the arts
- clergy
- consultant
- designer
- dietician
- editor
- educator

- filmmaker
- human resources
- journalist
- legal guardian
- librarian
- life coach
- mediator
- paramedic
- physician
- physiotherapist
- photographer
- project coordinator
- psychologist
- physiotherapist
- rehabilitation
- scientist
- social welfare
- sociologist
- teacher
- television producer
- therapist
- writer

Potential strengths and weaknesses

Like any other personality type, *mentors* have their potential strengths and weaknesses and this potential can be cultivated in a variety of ways. *Mentors'* personal happiness and professional fulfilment depend on whether they make the most of the 'pluses' offered by their personality type and face up to its inherent dangers. Here, then, is a SUMMARY of those 'pluses' and dangers:

Potential strengths

Mentors perceive things which are far from evident to others, seeing the connections between disparate events and repeated patterns of behaviour. When working to solve problems, they analyse the situation from various angles and different perspectives and have the ability to look ahead and identify future potential, possibilities and dangers. Their ideas are highly creative and unconventional and they have an excellent grasp of complex theories and abstract concepts.

They forge natural, sincere and profound interpersonal relationships, being genuinely interested in other people and their problems and sensitive to their feelings and needs. Characterised by their extraordinary intuition, empathy and natural warm-heartedness, they are splendid observers and listeners, capable of reading the feelings and emotions of others, inspiring them to discover and make the most of their potential and motivating them to take responsibility for their own lives.

Mentors strive for perfection and are able to penetrate beneath the surface of problems and identify their essence. When they see the sense of their work, they are capable of focusing on the task or matter in hand and are ready to make numerous sacrifices in devoting themselves to it. Conscientious and responsible, they treat any and every task they undertake seriously and are incapable of consciously working to anything less than their full ability. Indeed, given their desire to see everyone make the most of their potential and talents, they are extremely demanding of themselves and others alike. As past masters of the spoken and written word, they are able to express their thoughts clearly and comprehensibly.

Potential weaknesses

Mentors' idealism means that they often have trouble functioning in the real world and can be rather unfocused; for instance, when discussing a problem, they may well diverge from the matter in hand, drifting into considerations of a more general nature. They also struggle with everyday, routine activities and are inclined to forget details.

Their expectations of others can be unrealistic and may fail to make allowances for people's natural limitations, a tendency which often gives the impression that they are impossible to satisfy. As a rule, they assume that they are right, often not even offering an explanation of the basis for that conviction. They are also prone to dismissing other people's views in advance, without trying to hear them out. Their multilayered perception of reality often causes them to reflect on the rightness of the road they have chosen and the decisions they have made. They are frequently at a loss in situations requiring improvisation or rapid decisions.

Sharing their problems with others and accepting their help comes hard to them, as does coping in situations of conflict. They handle criticism very badly, often taking it as a personal attack and they respond poorly to stress, which drives them into a state of internal tension, frequently triggering somatic symptoms and depriving them of their faith in their own capabilities; indeed, at times, they will even turn to using substances.

Mentors are not only highly sensitive and easily hurt, but can also struggle to forgive, and may well go on nursing their injuries for a long time.

Personal development

Mentors' personal development depends on the extent to which they make use of their natural potential and surmount the dangers inherent in their personality type. What follows are some practical tips which, together, form a specific guide that we might call *The Mentor's Ten Commandments*.

Talk to people about your ideas

Not everyone will know how you came up with an idea, so why assume that it's obvious? Talking it over with your nearest and dearest or your colleagues not only does wonders for the atmosphere, but will also help you view it from a new perspective.

Stop fearing criticism

Quell your fear of expressing your own critical opinions and of accepting criticism from others. Criticism can be constructive. There is no law which says that it has to mean attacking people or undermining their worth.

Be more practical

You have a natural inclination to come up with idealistic notions which sometimes have little in common with real life. Give some thought to the practical aspects and to how they can actually be accomplished in this imperfect world we live in.

Stop dismissing other people's ideas and opinions

Listen carefully to what people have to say and try to understand their ideas before you dismiss them or announce that you have heard them before. Avoid assuming that no one else knows as much about a given matter as you do; this, in itself, is a mistake!

Stop being afraid of conflict

Conflicts do arise sometimes, even in our closest circles. They need not necessarily be destructive, though. In fact, they very often help us to uncover problems and solve them! So, when conflicts emerge, stop hiding your head in the sand and, instead, express your point of view and feelings about the situation openly.

Stop blaming others for your problems

Give some serious thought to where they spring from. Oversights and mistakes are not things that only happen to others. You, too, can be the root of a problem.

Stop conjuring up dark scenarios

Turn your focus away from threats and dangers. The fear they engender can become paralysing. Worry less and do more! Concentrate on life's brighter aspects and try to make the most of their potential.

Be more understanding

Show more patience towards other people's weaknesses and shortcomings. Remember that not everyone should be assigned the same tasks, because not everyone is skilled in the same fields. People's deficiencies are not manifestations of their ill-will, disinclination or laziness.

Take some time out

Try to get away from your responsibilities and duties once in a while and do something for the sheer pleasure, relaxation and fun of it. It will help you get a better perspective on things and you'll go back to your tasks with your mind and thinking refreshed.

Admit that you can make mistakes

None of us is infallible. Other people might well be absolutely right or partially right and you might be partially or absolutely wrong. Accept that fact and learn to admit your mistakes.

Well-known figures

Below is a list of some well-known people who match the *mentor's* profile:

- **Johann Wolfgang von Goethe** (1749-1832); the greatest German writer of the Classical period, whose poems, plays and prose works include *The ErlKing*, *Faust* and *The Sorrows of Young Werther* respectively, he was also a scholar and statesman.

- **Nathaniel Hawthorne** (1804-1864); one of America's greatest novelists and short story writers and a representative of Romanticism and transcendental philosophy, his works include *The Scarlet Letter*.

- **Emily Jane Brontë** (1818-1848); an English author and poet whose works include *Wuthering Heights*.

- **Fanny Crosby** (Frances Jane Crosby; 1820-1915); an American mission worker, poet, lyricist and composer who went blind shortly after birth, she was the author of more than eight thousand hymns and gospel songs and became one of the best-known women in the USA during her lifetime.

- **Mary Baker Eddy** (1821-1910); an American mystic, she was the founder of the Christian Science movement.

- **Mahatma Ghandi** (Mohandas Karamchand Gandhi; 1869-1948); one of the founders of the modern Indian state, he both supported and employed passive resistance as a tool for political struggle.

- **Nelson Mandela** (1918-2013); an activist in the cause of ending racial segregation in the Republic of South Africa, he went on to become the country's president and was awarded the Nobel Peace Prize.

- **Jimmy Carter** (James Earl Carter; born in 1924); the 39th president of the United States, an international activist in the cause of human rights and a holder of the Nobel Peace Prize.

- **Martin Luther King, Junior** (1929-1968); an American Baptist minister and activist in the cause of ending racial discrimination, he was awarded the Nobel Peace Prize.

- **Piers Anthony** (Piers Anthony Dillingham Jacob; born in 1934); an American science fiction and fantasy writer whose works include *Xanth*.

- **Michael Landon** (Eugene Maurice Orowitz; 1936-1991); an American screen actor, writer, director and producer whose filmography includes *Highway to Heaven*.

- **Billy Crystal** (William Edward Crystal; born in 1948); an American screen actor, director, writer and entertainer whose filmography includes *Analyze This*.

- **Mel Gibson** (Mel Columcille Gerard Gibson; born in 1956); an American screen actor whose roles include *Lethal Weapon*, he is also a director and producer with productions such as *The Passion of Christ* to his name.

- **Nicole Kidman** (born in 1967); an Australian-American screen actress and producer whose filmography includes *Cold Mountain*, she is also a singer and a UNICEF Goodwill Ambassador.

The ID16™© Personality Types in a Nutshell

The Administrator (ESTJ)

Life motto: We'll get the job done!

Administrators are hard-working, responsible and extremely loyal. Energetic and decisive, they value order, stability, security and clear rules. They are matter-of-fact and businesslike, logical, rational and practical and possess the capability to assimilate large amounts of detailed information.

Superb organisers, they are intolerant of ineffectuality, wastefulness and slothfulness. True to their convictions and direct in their contact with others, they present their point of view decisively and openly express critical opinions, sometimes hurting other people as a result.

The *administrator*'s four natural inclinations:

- source of life energy: the exterior world
- mode of assimilating information: via the senses
- decision-making mode: the mind
- lifestyle: organised

Similar personality types:

- the Animator
- the Inspector
- the Practitioner

Statistical data:

- *administrators* constitute between ten and thirteen per cent of the global community
- men predominate among *administrators* (60 per cent)
- the United States is an example of a nation corresponding to the *administrator's* profile[3]

Find out more!

The Administrator. Your Guide to the ESTJ Personality Type by Jaroslaw Jankowski

---

[3] What this means is not that all the residents of the USA fall within this personality type, but that American society as a whole possesses a great many of the character traits typical of the *administrator*.

The Advocate (ESFJ)

Life motto: How can I help you?

Advocates are well-organised, energetic and enthusiastic. Practical, responsible and conscientious, they are sincere and exceptionally gregarious.

Advocates are perceptive of human feelings, emotions and needs. They value harmony and find criticism and conflict difficult to bear. With their sensitivity to any and every manifestation of injustice, prejudice or detriment to another, they are genuinely interested in other people's problems and take real delight in helping them and tending to their needs, while often neglecting their own. They have a tendency to do everything for others and can be vulnerable to manipulation.

The *advocate*'s four natural inclinations:

- source of life energy: the exterior world
- mode of assimilating information: via the senses
- decision-making mode: the heart
- lifestyle: organised

Similar personality types:

- the Presenter
- the Protector
- the Artist

Statistical data:

- *advocates* constitute between ten and thirteen per cent of the global community
- women predominate among *advocates* (70 per cent)
- Canada is an example of a nation corresponding to the *advocate's* profile

Find out more!

The Advocate. Your Guide to the ESFJ Personality Type by Jaroslaw Jankowski

The Animator (ESTP)

Life motto: Let's DO something!

Animators are energetic, active and enterprising. Fond of the company of others, they have the ability to enjoy the moment and are spontaneous, flexible and open to change.

Animators are inspirers and instigators, spurring others to act. Being logical, rational and pragmatic realists, they are wearied by abstract concepts and solutions for the future. Their focus is on solving concrete problems in the here and now. They have difficulties with organising and planning and can be impulsive, acting first and thinking later.

The *animator's* four natural inclinations:

- source of life energy: the exterior world
- mode of assimilating information: via the senses

- decision-making mode: the mind
- lifestyle: spontaneous

Similar personality types:

- the Administrator
- the Practitioner
- the Inspector

Statistical data:

- *animators* constitute between six and ten per cent of the global community
- men predominate among *animators* (60 per cent)
- Australia is an example of a nation corresponding to the *animator's* profile

Find out more!

The Animator. Your Guide to the ESTP Personality Type by Jaroslaw Jankowski

The Artist (ISFP)

Life motto: Let's create something!

Artists are sensitive, creative and original, with a sense of the aesthetic and natural artistic talents. Independent in character, they follow their own system of values and are optimistic in outlook, with a positive approach to life and an ability to enjoy the moment.

Helping others is a source of joy to them. They find abstract theories tedious and would rather create reality than talk about it, although starting on something new comes more easily to them than finishing what they have already started. They have difficulty in voicing their own desires and needs.

The *artist's* four natural inclinations:

- source of life energy: the interior world
- mode of assimilating information: via the senses
- decision-making mode: the heart
- lifestyle: spontaneous

Similar personality types:

- the Protector
- the Presenter
- the Advocate

Statistical data:

- *artists* constitute between six and nine per cent of the global community
- women predominate among *artists* (60 per cent)
- China is an example of a nation corresponding to the *artist's* profile

Find out more!

The Artist. Your Guide to the ISFP Personality Type by Jaroslaw Jankowski

The Counsellor (ENFJ)

Life motto: My friends are my world

Counsellors are optimistic, enthusiastic and quick-witted. Courteous and tactful, they have an extraordinary gift for empathy and find joy in acting for the good of others, with no thought of themselves. They have the ability to influence other people, inspiring them, eliciting their hidden potential and giving them faith in their own powers. Radiating warmth, they draw others to them and often help them in solving their personal problems.

Counsellors can be over-trusting and have a tendency to view the world through rose-tinted glasses. With their focus on other people, they often forget about their own needs.

The *counsellor's* four natural inclinations:

- source of life energy: the exterior world
- mode of assimilating information: intuition
- decision-making mode: the heart
- lifestyle: organised

Similar personality types:

- the Enthusiast
- the Mentor
- the Idealist

Statistical data:

- *counsellors* constitute between three and five per cent of the global community
- women predominate among *counsellors* (80 per cent)
- France is an example of a nation corresponding to the *counsellor's* profile

Find out more!

The Counsellor. Your Guide to the ENFJ Personality Type by Jaroslaw Jankowski

The Director (ENTJ)

Life motto: I'll tell you what you need to do.

Directors are independent, active and decisive. Rational, logical and creative, when they analyse problems they look at the wider picture and are able to foresee the future consequences of human activities. They are characterised by optimism and a healthy sense of their own worth and are capable of transforming theoretical concepts into concrete, practical plans of action.

Visionaries, mentors and organisers, *directors* possess natural leadership skills. Their powerful personalities and direct and critical style can often have an intimidating effect, causing them problems in their interpersonal relationships.

The *director's* four natural inclinations:

- source of life energy: the exterior world

- mode of assimilating information: intuition
- decision-making mode: the mind
- lifestyle: organised

Similar personality types:

- the Innovator
- the Strategist
- the Logician

Statistical data:

- *directors* constitute between two and five per cent of the global community
- men predominate among *directors* (70 per cent)
- Holland is an example of a nation corresponding to the *director's* profile

Find out more!

The Director. Your Guide to the ENTJ Personality Type by Jaroslaw Jankowski

The Enthusiast (ENFP)

Life motto: We'll manage!

Enthusiasts are energetic, enthusiastic and optimistic. Capable of enjoying life and looking ahead to the future, they are dynamic, quick-witted and creative. They have a liking for people in general, value honest and genuine relationships and are warm, sincere and emotional. Criticism is something they handle badly. With their gift for empathy and ability to perceive people's needs, feelings and motives, they both inspire others and infect them with their own enthusiasm.

They love to be at the centre of events and are flexible and capable of improvising. Their inclination leads towards idealistic notions. Being easily distracted, they have problems with seeing things through to the end.

The *enthusiast's* four natural inclinations:

- source of life energy: the exterior world
- mode of assimilating information: intuition
- decision-making mode: the heart
- lifestyle: spontaneous

Similar personality types:

- the Counsellor
- the Idealist
- the Mentor

Statistical data:

- *enthusiasts* constitute between five and eight per cent of the global community
- women predominate among *enthusiasts* (60 per cent)
- Italy is an example of a nation corresponding to the *enthusiast's* profile

Find out more!

The Enthusiast. Your Guide to the ENFP Personality Type by Jaroslaw Jankowski

The Idealist (INFP)

Life motto: We CAN live differently.

Idealists are sensitive, loyal, and creative. Living in accordance with the values they hold is of immense importance to them and they both manifest an interest in the reality of the spirit and delve deeply into the mysteries of life. Wrapped up in the world's problems and open to the needs of other people, they prize harmony and balance.

Idealists are romantic; not only are they able to show love, but they also need warmth and affection themselves. With their outstanding ability to read other people's feelings and emotions, they build healthy, profound and enduring relationships. They feel that they are on very shaky ground in situations of conflict and have no real resistance to stress and criticism.

The *idealist's* four natural inclinations:

- source of life energy: the interior world
- mode of assimilating information: intuition
- decision-making mode: the heart
- lifestyle: spontaneous

Similar personality types:

- the Mentor
- the Enthusiast
- the Counsellor

Statistical data:

- *idealists* constitute between one and four per cent of the global community
- women predominate among *idealists* (60 per cent)
- Thailand is an example of a nation corresponding to the *idealist's* profile

Find out more!

The Idealist. Your Guide to the INFP Personality Type by Jaroslaw Jankowski

The Innovator (ENTP)

Life motto: How about trying a different approach...?

Innovators are inventive, original and independent. Optimistic, energetic and enterprising, they are people of action who love being at the centre of events and solving 'insoluble' problems. Their thoughts are turned to the future and they are curious about the world and visionary by nature. Open to new concepts and ideas, they enjoy new experiences and experiments and have the ability to identify the connections between separate events.

Innovators are spontaneous, communicative and self-assured. However, they tend to overestimate their own possibilities and have problems with seeing things through to the end. They are also inclined to be impatient and to take risks.

The *innovator's* four natural inclinations:

- source of life energy: the exterior world
- mode of assimilating information: intuition
- decision-making mode: the mind
- lifestyle: spontaneous

Similar personality types:

- the Director
- the Logician
- the Strategist

Statistical data:

- *innovators* constitute between three and five per cent of the global community
- men predominate among *innovators* (70 per cent)
- Israel is an example of a nation corresponding to the *innovator's* profile

Find out more!

The Innovator. Your Guide to the ENTP Personality Type by Jaroslaw Jankowski

The Inspector (ISTJ)

Life motto: *Duty first.*

Inspectors are people who can always be counted on. Well-mannered, punctual, reliable, conscientious and responsible, when they give their word, they keep it. Being analytical, methodical, systematic and logical by nature, they tend be seen as serious, cold and reserved. They prize calm, stability and order, have no fondness for change and like clear principles and concrete rules.

Inspectors are hard-working, persevering and capable of seeing things through to the end. As perfectionists, they try to exercise control over everything within their sphere and are sparing in their praise. They also underrate the importance of other people's feelings and emotions.

The *inspector's* four natural inclinations:

- source of life energy: the interior world
- mode of assimilating information: via the senses
- decision-making mode: the mind
- lifestyle: organised

Similar personality types:

- the Practitioner
- the Administrator
- the Animator

Statistical data:

- *inspectors* constitute between six and ten per cent of the global community
- men predominate among *inspectors* (60 per cent)
- Switzerland is an example of a nation corresponding to the *inspector's* profile

Find out more!

The Inspector. Your Guide to the ISTJ Personality Type by Jaroslaw Jankowski

The Logician (INTP)

Life motto: Above all else, seek to discover the truths about the world.

Logicians are original, resourceful and creative. With a love for solving problems of a theoretical nature, they are analytical, quick-witted, enthusiastically disposed towards new concepts and have the ability to connect individual phenomena, educing general rules and theories from them. Logical, exact and inquiring, they are quick to spot incoherence and inconsistency.

Logicians are independent, sceptical of existing solutions and authorities, tolerant and open to new challenges. When immersed in thought, they will sometimes lose touch with the outside world.

The *logician's* four natural inclinations:

- source of life energy: the interior world

- mode of assimilating information: intuition
- decision-making mode: the mind
- lifestyle: spontaneous

Similar personality types:

- the Strategist
- the Innovator
- the Director

Statistical data:

- *logicians* constitute between two and three per cent of the global community;
- men predominate among *logicians* (80 per cent)
- India is an example of a nation corresponding to the *logician's* profile

Find out more!

The Logician. Your Guide to the INTP Personality Type by Jaroslaw Jankowski

The Mentor (INFJ)

Life motto: The world CAN be a better place!

Mentors are creative and sensitive. With their gaze fixed firmly on the future, they spot opportunities and potential imperceptible to others. Idealists and visionaries, they are geared towards helping people and are conscientious, responsible and, at one and the same time, courteous, caring and friendly. They strive to understand the mechanisms governing the world and view problems from a wide perspective.

Superb listeners and observers, *mentors* are characterised by their extraordinary empathy, intuition and trust of people and are capable of reading the feelings and emotions of others. They find criticism and conflict difficult to bear and can come across as enigmatic.

The *mentor's* four natural inclinations:

- source of life energy: the interior world
- mode of assimilating information: intuition
- decision-making mode: the heart
- lifestyle: organised

Similar personality types:

- the Idealist
- the Counsellor
- the Enthusiast

Statistical data:

- *mentors* constitute one per cent of the global community and are the most rarely occurring of the sixteen personality types
- women predominate among *mentors* (80 per cent)
- Norway is an example of a nation corresponding to the *mentor's* profile

Find out more!

The Mentor. Your Guide to the INFJ Personality Type
by Jaroslaw Jankowski

The Practitioner (ISTP)

Life motto: Actions speak louder than words.

Practitioners are optimistic and spontaneous, with a positive approach to life. Reserved and independent, they hold true to their personal convictions and view external principles and norms with scepticism. They find abstract concepts and solutions for the future tiresome and would far rather roll up their sleeves and get to work on solving tangible and concrete problems.

Adapting well to new places and situations, they enjoy fresh challenges and risks and are capable of keeping a cool head in the face of threats and danger. Their general reticence and extreme reserve when it comes to expressing their opinions mean that other people may often find them impenetrable.

The *practitioner's* four natural inclinations:

- source of life energy: the interior world
- mode of assimilating information: via the senses
- decision-making mode: the mind
- lifestyle: spontaneous

Similar personality types:

- the Inspector
- the Animator
- the Administrator

Statistical data:

- *practitioners* constitute between six and nine per cent of the global community
- men predominate among *practitioners* (60 per cent)
- Singapore is an example of a nation corresponding to the *practitioner's* profile

Find out more!

The Practitioner. Your Guide to the ISTP Personality Type by Jaroslaw Jankowski

The Presenter (ESFP)

Life motto: Now is the perfect moment!

Presenters are optimistic, energetic and outgoing, with the ability to enjoy life and have fun to the full. Practical, flexible and spontaneous at one and the same time, they enjoy change and new experiences, coping badly with solitude, stagnation and routine.

With their liking for being at the centre of attention, they are natural-born actors and their speaking abilities arouse the interest and enthusiasm of their listeners. Focused as they are on the present moment, they will sometimes lose sight of their long-term aims and can also have problems with foreseeing the consequences of their actions.

The *presenter's* four natural inclinations:

- source of life energy: the exterior world
- mode of assimilating information: via the senses
- decision-making mode: the heart
- lifestyle: spontaneous

Similar personality types:

- the Advocate
- the Artist
- the Protector

Statistical data:

- *presenters* constitute between eight and thirteen per cent of the global community
- women predominate among *presenters* (60 per cent)
- Brazil is an example of a nation corresponding to the *presenter's* profile

Find out more!

The Presenter. Your Guide to the ESFP Personality Type by Jaroslaw Jankowski

The Protector (ISFJ)

Life motto: Your happiness matters to me.

Protectors are sincere, warm-hearted, unassuming, trustworthy and extraordinarily loyal. With their ability to perceive people's needs and their desire to help them, they will always put others first. Practical, well-organised and gifted with both an eye and a memory for detail, they are responsible, hard-working, patient, persevering and capable of seeing things through to the end.

Protectors set great store by tranquillity, stability and friendly relations with others and are skilled at building bridges between people. By the same token, they find conflict and criticism difficult to bear. Given their powerful sense of duty and their constant readiness to come to the aid of others, they can end up being used by people.

The *protector's* four natural inclinations:

- source of life energy: the interior world
- mode of assimilating information: via the senses
- decision-making mode: the heart
- lifestyle: organised

Similar personality types:

- the Artist
- the Advocate
- the Presenter

Statistical data:

- *protectors* constitute between eight and twelve per cent of the global population
- women predominate among *protectors* (70 per cent)
- Sweden is an example of a nation corresponding to the *protector's* profile

Find out more!

The Protector. Your Guide to the ISFJ Personality Type by Jaroslaw Jankowski

The Strategist (INTJ)

Life motto: I can certainly improve this.

Strategists are independent and outstandingly individualistic, with an immense seam of inner energy. Creative, inventive and resourceful, others perceive them as competent, self-assured and, at one and the same time, distant and enigmatic. No matter what they turn their attention to, they will always look at the bigger picture and they have a driving urge to improve the world around them and set it in order.

Well-organised, responsible, critical and demanding, they are difficult to knock off balance – and just as hard to please to the full. Reading the emotions and feelings of others is something they find very problematic.

The *strategist's* four natural inclinations:

- source of life energy: the interior world
- mode of assimilating information: intuition
- decision-making mode: the mind
- lifestyle: organised

Similar personality types:

- the Logician
- the Director
- the Innovator

Statistical data:

- *strategists* constitute between one and two per cent of the global community
- men predominate among *strategists* (80 per cent)
- Finland is an example of a nation corresponding to the *strategist's* profile

Find out more!

The Strategist. Your Guide to the INTJ Personality Type by Jaroslaw Jankowski

Additional information

The four natural inclinations

1. THE DOMINANT SOURCE OF LIFE ENERGY

   a. THE EXTERIOR WORLD
   People who draw their energy from outside. They need activity and contact with others and find being alone for any length of time hard to bear.

   b. THE INTERIOR WORLD
   People who draw their energy from their inner world. They need quiet and solitude and feel drained

when they spend any length of time in a group.

2. THE DOMINANT MODE OF ASSIMILATING INFORMATION

a. VIA THE SENSES

People who rely on the five senses and are persuaded by facts and evidence. They have a liking for methods and practices which are tried and tested and prefer concrete tasks and are realists who trust in experience.

b. VIA INTUITION

People who rely on the sixth sense and are driven by what they 'feel in their bones'. They have a liking for innovative solutions and problems of a theoretical nature and are characterised by a creative approach to their tasks and the ability to predict.

3. THE DOMINANT DECISION-MAKING MODE

a. THE MIND

People who are guided by logic and objective principles. They are critical and direct in expressing their opinions.

b. THE HEART
    People who are guided by their
    feelings and values. They long for
    harmony and mutual
    understanding with others.

4. THE DOMINANT LIFESTYLE

a. ORGANISED
    People who are conscientious and
    organised. They value order and
    like to operate according to plan.

b. SPONTANEOUS
    People who are spontaneous and
    value freedom of action. They live
    for the moment and have no
    trouble finding their feet in new
    situations.

The approximate percentage of each personality type in the world population

Personality Type:	Proportion:
• The Administrator (ESTJ):	10-13%
• The Advocate (ESFJ):	10-13%
• The Animator (ESTP):	6-10%
• The Artist (ISFP):	6-9%
• The Counsellor (ENFJ):	3-5 %
• The Director (ENTJ):	2-5%

- The Enthusiast (ENFP):   5-8%
- The Idealist (INFP):   1-4%
- The Innovator (ENTP):   3-5%
- The Inspector (ISTJ):   6-10%
- The Logician (INTP):   2-3%
- The Mentor (INFJ):   ca. 1%
- The Practitioner (ISTP):   6-9%
- The Presenter (ESFP):   8-13%
- The Protector (ISFJ):   8-12%
- The Strategist (INTJ):   1-2%

The approximate percentage of women and men of each personality type in the world population

Personality Type:	Women / Men:
The Administrator (ESTJ):	40% / 60%
The Advocate (ESFJ):	70% / 30%
The Animator (ESTP):	40% / 60%
The Artist (ISFP):	60% / 40%
The Counsellor (ENFJ):	80% / 20%
The Director (ENTJ):	30% / 70%
The Enthusiast (ENFP):	60% / 40%
The Idealist (INFP):	60% / 40%
The Innovator (ENTP):	30% / 70%
The Inspector (ISTJ):	40% / 60%
The Logician (INTP):	20% / 80%
The Mentor (INFJ):	80% / 20%
The Practitioner (ISTP):	40% / 60%
The Presenter (ESFP):	60% / 40%

- The Protector (ISFJ):   70% / 30%
- The Strategist (INTJ):   20% / 80%

Bibliography

- Arraj, Tyra & Arraj, James: *Tracking the Elusive Human, Volume 1: A Practical Guide to C.G. Jung's Psychological Types, W.H. Sheldon's Body and Temperament Types and Their Integration*, Inner Growth Books, 1988
- Arraj, James: *Tracking the Elusive Human, Volume 2: An Advanced Guide to the Typological Worlds of C. G. Jung, W.H. Sheldon, Their Integration, and the Biochemical Typology of the Future*, Inner Growth Books, 1990
- Berens, Linda V.; Cooper, Sue A.; Ernst, Linda K.; Martin, Charles R.; Myers, Steve; Nardi, Dario; Pearman, Roger R.; Segal, Marci; Smith, Melissa: *A Quick Guide to the 16 Personality Types in Organizations: Understanding Personality Differences in the Workplace*, Telos Publications, 2002

- Geier, John G. & Downey, E. Dorothy: *Energetics of Personality*, Aristos Publishing House, 1989

- Hunsaker, Phillip L. & Alessandra, Anthony J.: *The Art of Managing People*, Simon and Schuster, 1986

- Jung, Carl Gustav: *Psychological Types (The Collected Works of C. G. Jung, Vol. 6)*, Princeton University Press, 1976

- Kise, Jane A. G.; Stark, David & Krebs Hirsch, Sandra: *LifeKeys: Discover Who You Are*, Bethany House, 2005

- Kroeger, Otto & Thuesen, Janet: *Type Talk or How to Determine Your Personality Type and Change Your Life*, Delacorte Press, 1988

- Lawrence, Gordon: *People Types and Tiger Stripes*, Center for Applications of Psychological Type, 1993

- Lawrence, Gordon: *Looking at Type and Learning Styles*, Center for Applications of Psychological Type, 1997

- Maddi, Salvatore R.: *Personality Theories: A Comparative Analysis*, Waveland, 2001

- Martin, Charles R.: *Looking at Type: The Fundamentals Using Psychological Type To Understand and Appreciate Ourselves and Others*, Center for Applications of Psychological Type, 2001

- Meier C.A.: Personality: *The Individuation Process in the Light of C. G. Jung's Typology*, Daimon Verlag, 2007

- Pearman, Roger R. & Albritton, Sarah: *I'm Not Crazy, I'm Just Not You: The Real Meaning of the Sixteen Personality Types*, Davies-Black Publishing, 1997
- Segal, Marci: Creativity and Personality Type: *Tools for Understanding and Inspiring the Many Voices of Creativity*, Telos Publications, 2001
- Sharp, Daryl: Personality Type: *Jung's Model of Typology*, Inner City Books, 1987
- Spoto, Angelo: *Jung's Typology in Perspective*, Chiron Publications, 1995
- Tannen, Deborah: *You Just Don't Understand*, William Morrow and Company, 1990
- Thomas, Jay C. & Segal, Daniel L.: *Comprehensive Handbook of Personality and Psychopathology, Personality and Everyday Functioning*, Wiley, 2005
- Thomson, Lenore: *Personality Type: An Owner's Manual*, Shambhala, 1998
- Tieger, Paul D. & Barron-Tieger Barbara: *Just Your Type: Create the Relationship You've Always Wanted Using the Secrets of Personality Type*, Little, Brown and Company, 2000
- Von Franz, Marie-Louise & Hillman, James: *Lectures on Jung's Typology*, Continuum International Publishing Group, 1971

Putting the Reader first.

An Author Campaign Facilitated by ALLi